SMALL POOLS

Editor: Paco Asensio

Text: Fanny Tagavi

Photographies: Pere Planells

Art director: Mireia Casanovas Soley

Graphic design: Emma Termes Parera

Translation: Wendy Griswold

Proofreading: Julie King

2001 © Loft Publications s.l.

ISBN Softcover: 0-8230-4858-6

ISBN Hardcover: 0-06-018588-0

D.L.: B-51.457-2000

Printed in Spain

Gràfiques Ibèria S.A.

2001 © Loft Publications S.L. and HBI,
an imprint of HarperCollins Publishers

First published in 2001 by LOFT and HBI,
an imprint of HarperCollins Publishers
10 East 53rd St. New York, NY 10022-5299
Distributed in the U.S. and Canada by Watson-Guptill Publications
770 Broadway New York, NY 10003-9595 Telephone: (800) 451-1741
or (732) 363-4511 in NJ, AK, HI Fax: (732) 363-0338
Distributed throughout the rest of the world by
HarperCollins International
10 East 53rd St. New York, NY 10022-5299
Fax: (212) 207-7654

If you would like to suggest projects for inclusion in our next volumes,
please e-mail details to us at: loft@loftpublications.com

We have tried our best to contact all copyright holders.
In individual cases where this has not been possible,
we request copyright holders to get in touch with the publishing house.

POOLS

The term "pool" once meant a tub of water that could function as a storage tank, a fish hatchery, or, as we know it today, a place to swim. To discover the origins of pools, we must go back to Roman times. In the Roman house, the pool was the impluvium, or a kind of tank to collect rainwater. And in Roman cities near the sea, it was the vivarium, where fish intended for consumption were kept. As the limaria, the pool formed part of the aqueduct system for collecting and distributing water. Finally, and only in the thermae of Roman cities, was the natatorium, a swimming pool in the shape of a cistern. The garden pool became common in the early 17th Century, with the arrival of the baroque style, and lasted until the 19th Century. The garden pool´s purpose was mainly aesthetic: it provided visual and auditory enjoyment for the stroller seeking a source of reflection and inspiration in the domestic setting. Thus, the usage and meaning of the word "pool" have evolved slowly since antiquity, until it finally came to be known as a functional object, whether elegant, therapeutic, or simply recreational. However, there has been one constant, parallel element in the historical development of the pool. These are the thermae, among the oldest therapeutic systems in the world, which, according to some research, date back to the 2nd Century before the Christian era, with the construction of the Stabian Baths of Pompeii, the oldest still in existence. Thermae and public baths nearly disappeared when obscurantism arrived in central Europe in the Middle Ages and the Church spoke out against the ritual of the bath by proclaiming that spiritual purity took priority over physical cleanliness. Meanwhile, in the rest of Europe, and in Islamic and Middle Eastern societies, social, hygienic, and religious baths flourished. Architecturally, they consisted of a large central space with vaulted ceilings, heated by steam and surrounded by smaller rooms, decorated with marble or mosaics. Despite the passage of time and certain vicissitudes, the hama has not only survived, but has become common, even in sports complexes. Because of their ability to stimulate genuine physical and psychological well-being, we have included the designs of several hamams that have formally integrated the thermal bath and in which water, as a source of health, plays the starring role.

The pool as a representation of paradise

Over the years, the pool, as a unit of construction, evolved in accordance with architectural trends. But it was only in the mid-20th Century, with the appearance of new materials and construction systems, that man was really able to give free reign to his boundless imagination, creating, shaping, and molding his immediate environment. Hence the formal richness of the projects presented in this book, which all share a growing concern for the disappearance of ecological balance. This translates into great respect for the natural spaces where the water areas have been integrated. The projects merge perfectly with their surroundings, as a tribute to nature's generosity.

Man's creativity has made it possible to enter the transparent fluidity of a sheet of turquoise water that peeks out over a cliff; to visually connect with infinity by transforming a recess in the rocky skirt of an old quarry into a pool and luxuriant garden; or to simply recapture ancient eastern customs and practices. Materials, textures, shapes, and colors merge in a magnificent exercise in cultural and social architecture that cannot fail to impress. Architecture and emotion have always joined together to realize the human being's instinct for perfection.

Fanny Tagavi

Between a small plot of cropland and an orchard of young fruit trees, this swimming pool, located in Palma de Majorca, Spain, is framed by a row of rocks on which the patina of time has left its mark. Three mysterious steps invite the onlooker to enter the transparent fluidity of its water.

The swimming pool is associated with contemplation, a fresh pool flanked by a soft grassy area in deliberate contrast to the arid land surrounding it.

This project wisely used the elements of the country house to visually condition the space on different levels, in a manner similar to a three-dimensional picture. The original stones from the country home were used to divide the principal space into three areas: the swimming pool, the ancient treadmill, and a sunbathing zone on the upper level.

The old z-shaped retaining wall becomes a path and shelters the pool, originally a reservoir that collected water to irrigate the field. The small, tidy orchard still stretches, on a second level, to the foot of the pool, along with the remains of a small treadmill, recycled as a sculpture for contemplation, a silent witness to the past.

RECOVERING THE PAST

Location: **Majorca, Spain**
Surface area: **129 sq. ft.**

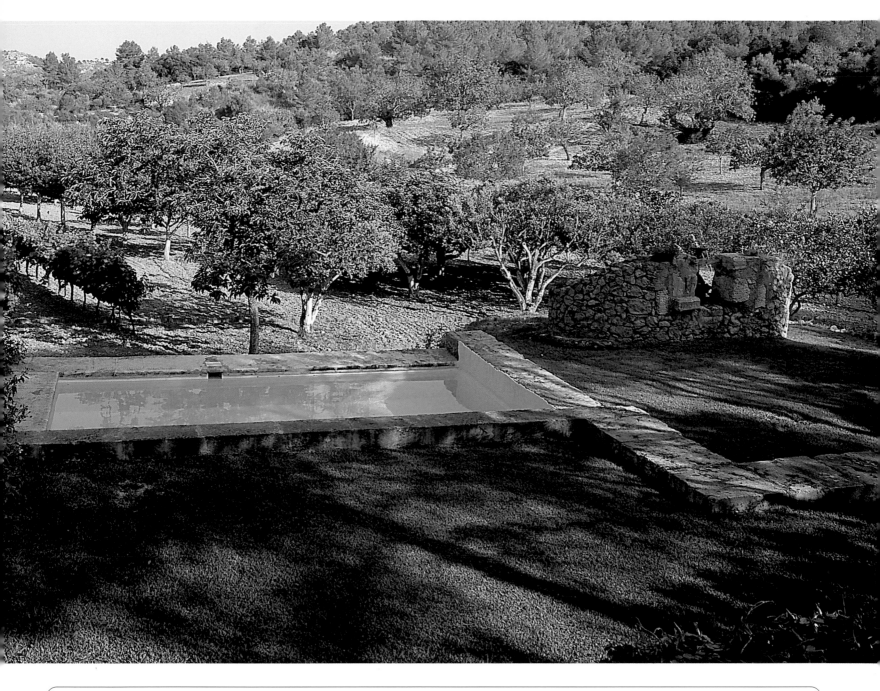

Panorama of the two areas that comprise the main level: the swimming pool and the old treadmill. On a second visual level, we see the orchard of young fruit trees.

A water deposit was converted into the pool. and is now protected by the charm of the nearby fruit trees.

This ancient reservoir, restored and converted into a swimming pool perfectly integrated with the original structure of the house, is sheltered by a 200 year old wall. The pool's charm comes from the bewitching turquoise color of its water and the ocher luminosity of antique wall that functions as the project's starting point.

To blend the pool's profile into its setting, a sandstone trim was chosen, whose sand color complements the rest of the materials. On one end, a small retaining wall, also covered with stones, becomes an informal diving board or sunbathing area. Behind it, lush vegetation flourishes, hiding a stone guest house from view.

The ends of the pool are characterized by very diverse landscaping: on one end, the color and splendor of freely-growing vegetation; on the other, the precision and simplicity of a monastic cloister. Thus two worlds with two landscape treatments are joined by a path with rounded edges, which runs rectilinear and parallel to the pool and sharply interrupts the green grass of a small orchard of fruit trees.

At the end of the path, a few steps down, a fountain offers strollers the coolness and musicality of its crystaline waters. The details were created to delight and soothe the senses through the power of nature's beauty and simplicity.

BETWEEN
TWO WORLDS

Location: **Tuscany, Italy**
Surface area: **161 sq. ft.**

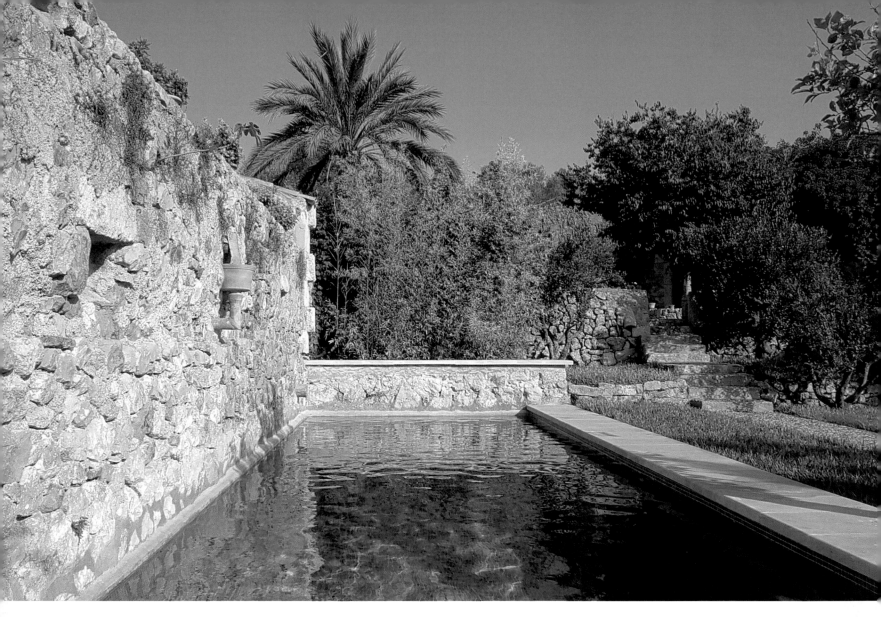

This rectangular pool trimmed with sand-colored stone is protected by a 200 year old wall. At the back, a low retaining wall serves as a diving board.

 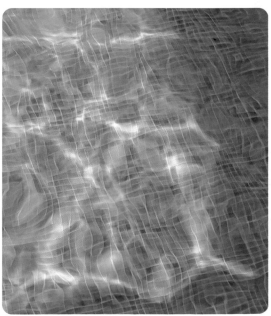

The inside of the pool is coated with green gresite so the water takes on a magnificent turquoise color which highlights the luminous ochre color of the ancient wall that shelters it.

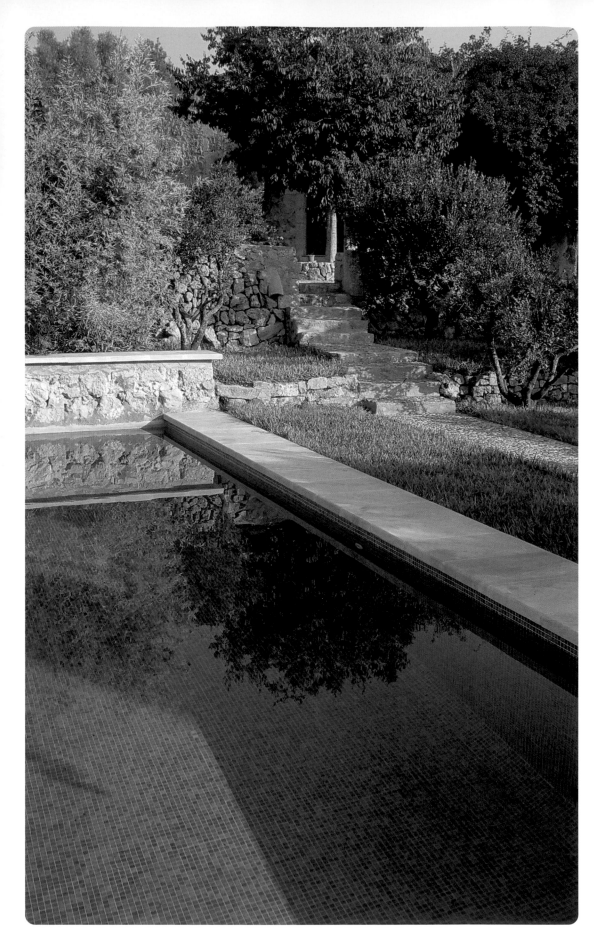

The chromatic play of the vegetation that grows freely hides a stone house for guests.

A path with rounded edges, rectilinear and parallel to the pool, interrupts the green grass of a small orchard of fruit trees.

Amid rocks cracked by the sun, rural fragrances, and the buzz of the grasshoppers, a smooth slope shelters low stone walls which were once used for terrace farming, a traditional system of agriculture. At its feet, as if at a stream bed, lies the emerald water of this pool, which combines artificial curves and rough shapes.

This project applied architectural criteria to the natural setting and achieved a perfect blending of both. All landscaping around the pool was rejected in order to maintain the strength of the earth and rock, in stark contrast to the colorful luminosity of the water. In accordance with this principle, the land needed for the pool was cleared, and the exterior perimeter was covered with a simple, wide stone strip.

The rocky side of the pool has a small platform that intensifies the feel of a stream and serves as a lounging area and natural diving board. A small, completely whitewashed well that provides fresh water is prominent. The mountainous slope serves as an informal entrance to the pool, which seems to be reinforced by the presence of steps in the shape of waves submerged in the water.

In this place of lights and contrast, the priority was to preserve the authentic appearance of the landscape without changing it; the setting had to remain the star player, without sacrificing the magnificent advantages of modern society.

A STREAM AMID THE ROCKS

Location: **Ibiza, Spain**
Surface area: **269 sq. ft.**

The originality of this pool lies in the incorporation of its rugged terrain as an integral part of the project. The construction criteria were blended with the setting, creating a pool shaped like a natural pond in the new grouping. A whitewashed well that provides fresh water overlooks the setting.

The contrast between the emerald color of the water and the ocher of the rock reinforces the sensation of being at a stream bed. Also, the incorporation of the rocky skirt into the pool keeps the water at the proper temperature all summer long.

This rectangular pool sits between two long, dry stone dividing walls and is surrounded by a soft tapestry of grass.

RURAL SYMMETRY

Location: **Santorini, Greece**
Surface area: **258 sq. ft.**

The principal goal of the design was to overcome the problems presented by the site, a narrow band surrounded by walls of varying heights. Therefore, its excessive linearity had to be compensated for and smaller areas had to be created on the two shorter sides, where the presence of small and medium-high walls physically and visually cut any expansion.

To break the rigidity of the straight lines and to add volume, the principal and older wall was used as support for dense vegetation that could spread out like a natural cascade. This vegetation, comprised mainly of a spectacular bougainvillea and various common plant species, softens the harshness of the dry stone and isolates the area, ensuring a peaceful, intimate setting.

A limestone rim puts the finishing touch on this sheet of calm water and houses the ingenious channels that return water to the pool to prevent the grass from flooding.

The end, located at the entrance to the open area, became an informal porch extending from a rear wall. A unique canopy makes this angular spot a pleasant niche, perfectly integrated into the space. On the opposite end, three steps break up the dividing wall while joining the two side walls. This solution, based on one material, stone, made it possible to construct a formally balanced area for sunbathing. Several stylized sun lounges of tropical wood complete the setting, and add a note of color.

Detail of the ochre canopy at the entrance to the open space. This pleasant corner, which serves as an informal porch extending from a rear wall, is carpeted with the same soft grass that covers the entire area.

The pool is located on a narrow strip surrounded by dividing walls of varying heights. The dense vegetation that spreads out over the dry stone like a natural cascade adds volume and breaks up the excessive formal linearity.

The placement and magnificent orientation of this swimming pool were two determining factors in this project. It is treated as a sheet of still water that creates a dialogue with the surroundings. The overall effect is one of an infinite mirror between the earth and sky.

The irregularly-shaped swimming pool, dotted with small peninsulas of rock, resembles a calm natural lake, a niche where one can find peace and primordial silence. In one of the corners, melting into the landscape, a tree trunk is visible, twisted by the passage of time and placed strategically for contemplation in accordance with the tenets of Zen philosophy. In this respect, the designers wanted to avoid overloading the space around the swimming pool, preferring to give a starring role to the splendid natural surroundings.

This infinity pool is edged with the same type of rock used for the small artificial peninsulas. This accentuates the natural, integrated feeling by avoiding a continuous, defined edge. The swimming pool was not intended to change the landscape, but to be a continuation of it. So the materials for the pool and the various areas surrounding the water are unified. These are at the same level as the water's surface, strengthening the visual continuity and the spectacular character of the landscape, which blends seamlessly with the main level of the swimming pool.

A MIRROR BETWEEN THE EARTH AND SKY

Location: **Majorca, Spain**
Surface area: **430 sq. ft.**

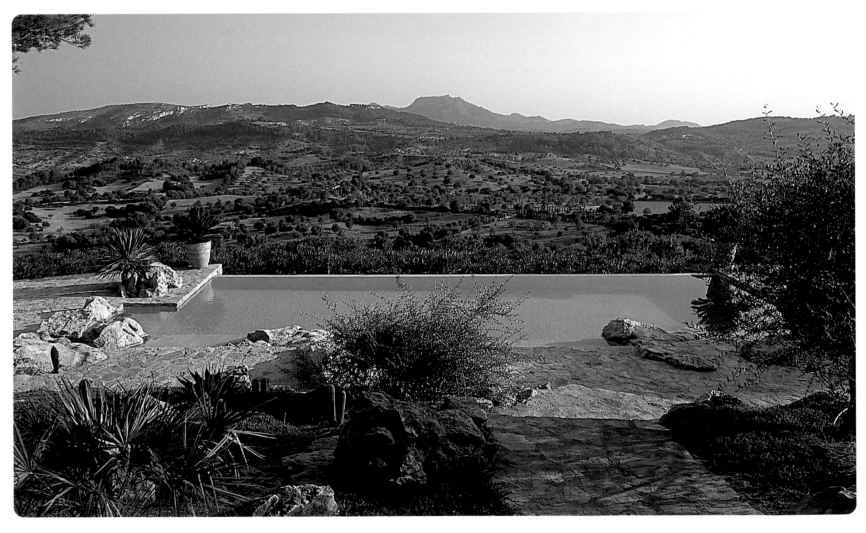

A key factor for integrating the pool naturally into its surroundings was to unify the materials as well as the different zones around it.

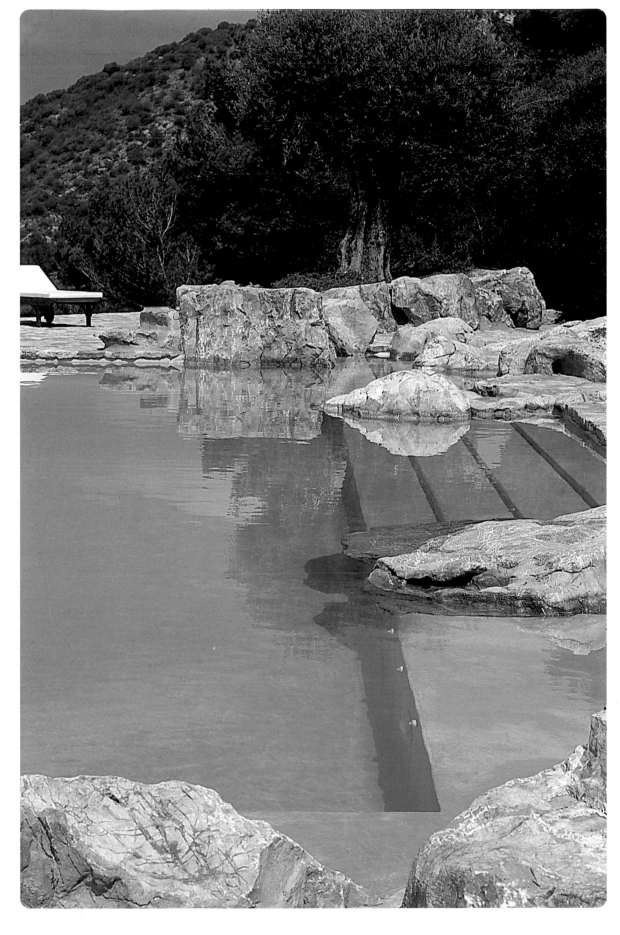

The twisted trunk of a tree that shows the passage of time is situated in a strategic position where it merges with the landscape. The tree obliges the onlooker to stop and contemplate it, in accordance with the guidelines of Zen philosophy.

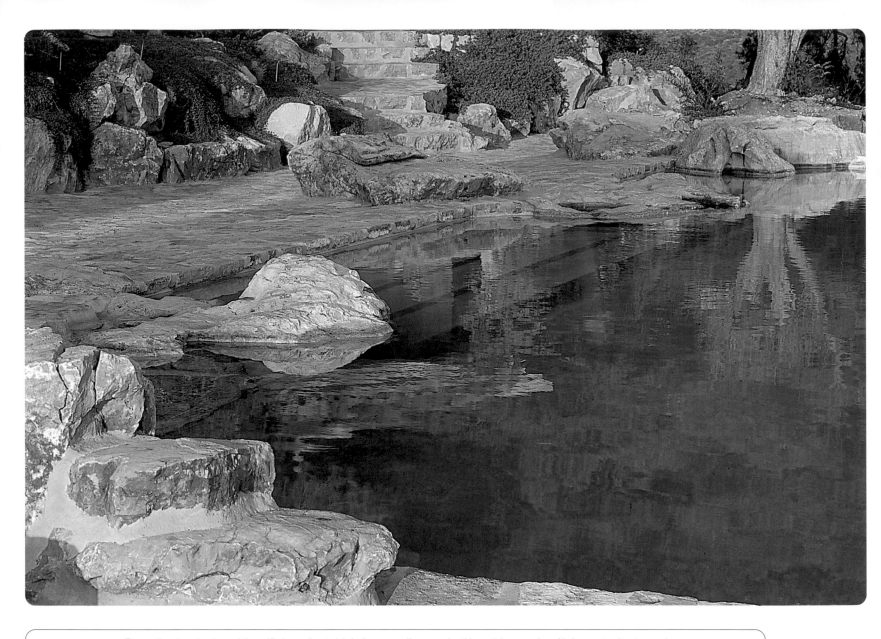

The small rock peninsulas and the unified use of materials in the surrounding area give this pool the sensation of being a natural water pond.

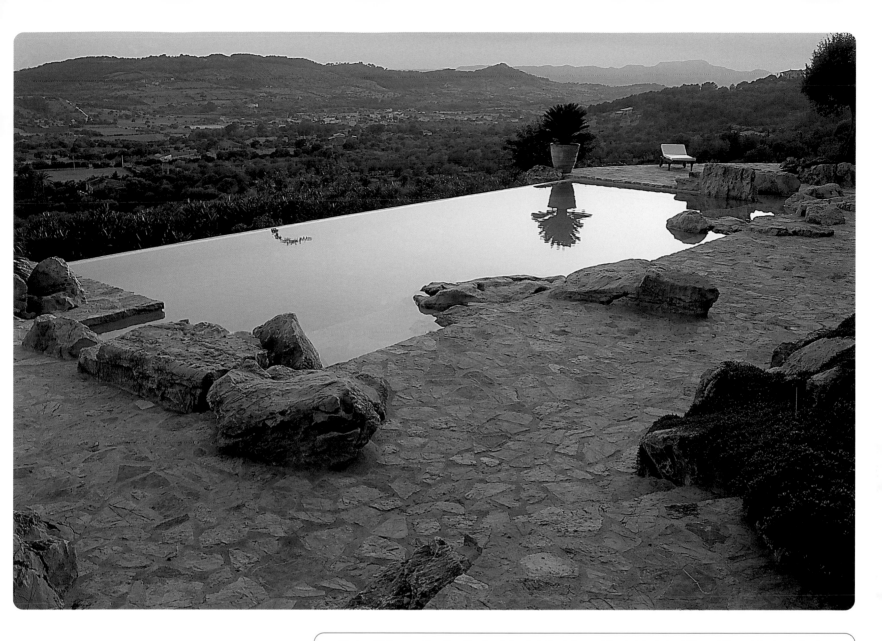

The beautiful perspective offered by the site´s orientation influenced the decision to treat this pool like a static sheet of water.

A small pond in the exotic intimacy of an interior Moroccan patio, this shallow pool is an example of how mosaics are still used in Morocco.

TRADITIONAL INSPIRATION

An elaborate, bright turquoise finish that acquires all its splendor from the sun's reflection crowns a bright border which extends around the entire interior perimeter of the pool. A soft salmon color covers the structure, creating a chromatic axis between the pool and the principal and side façades, which also boast Moroccan floor tiles and two magnificent wooden chairs that preside over the pool like ritual carvings. At a higher level,

steps covered in gresite the same color as the pool lead to a small terrace dominated by three arched windows. Wrought iron and wood furnishings decorate a breakfast / dinner nook with elegant simplicity.

This is a dynamic space conceived for intimacy, a design based on Moroccan decorative tradition, in which even the simplicity of a border stands out as a complex geometric exercise. Color and textures merge here to create a unique and aesthetically pleasing space.

Location: **Douar Abiat, Marrakech**
Surface area: **108 sq. ft.**

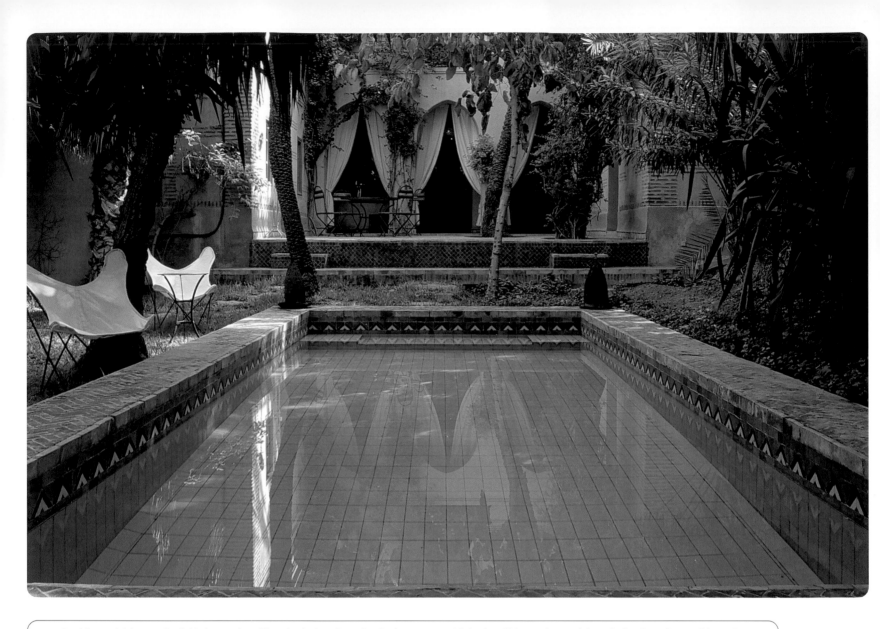

An elaborate, bright turquoise finish that acquires all its splendor from the sun's reflection crowns a plain border which extends around the entire interior perimeter of the pool.

The lateral façade houses a small, paved space with Moroccan tiles that is decorated with two magnificent wooden chairs that preside over the pool like ritual sculptures.

A cool, peaceful refuge, this small oasis emerges from the arid land that surrounds it. The geometric balance comes from the perfect relationship of its three volumes: the swimming pool, rectilinear and with a smooth surface of water, the terrace, and the main building, both just one story high. A stone wall of medium height, perfectly restored, joins the two structures and at the same time surrounds and delimits the entire property. In addition, it creates a dividing line between the property and the setting, based on color and a single texture, the roughness of the stone.

The visual perspectives from this line occur at any point, since the property and the adjacent land are at the same level. The intent was to bring out the play of contrasts resulting from the juxtaposition of the dry land and the artificial grass that surround the blue surface of the water.

The sense of continuity comes from the homogeneousness of the colors and from the materials used to restore the property and build the pool. The stone and the sand color become the chromatic base of the grouping, heightening awareness of the intense blue of the water and green of the vegetation.

The only vertical element, two regal palm trees, stand between the two structures, dominating the pool and breaking the infinite immensity of the sky. The evocative presence of these palms, as in a desert oasis, acts as a guide from the road.

COLOR
CONTRASTS

Location: **Majorca, Spain**
Surface area: **516 sq. ft.**

Detail of the bench inside the pool, which extends from side to side.

The porch, where the granary originally stood, opens up onto the pool, which is at the same level as the rest of the construction. The barbecue area can be seen next to the sofa.

The perimeter of the pool was built with natural stone of the same sand color as the wall that surrounds the property. The predominance of straight lines enhances the contrasting colors while making the pool a fluid mirror, perfectly integrated with the surroundings.

The only decorative element are wooden loungers whose refined style heightens the whiteness of the cushions.

THE REINTERPRETATION OF WATER

Location: **Marrakech, Morocco**
Surface area: **430 sq. ft.**

This magnificent, colorful pool, surrounded by a dense wall of vegetation, blends perfectly with its surrounding and emerges from the natural setting. A spectacular stepped entrance invites the visitor to slip into the therapeutic pleasure of the water and to enjoy the beauty of the landscape from a wide underwater bench.

The chromatic intensity of this pool, bright and cheerful, combined with the complex geometry of the double edging of fired clay that finishes off the edges, are a sampling of the craftsmanship still practiced today in Marrakech, where the property is located. The excellent glazed mosaic work on the central band of the small channel that divides the edging, and the various geometric finishes located both inside and outside the pool, are small samplings of the ornamental richness that has characterized this country for centuries.

On one end of the pool, symmetrically aligned at ground level, six slender jets of water are directly connected with the highest part of the pool, forming a unique fountain which is an integral part of the project.

Details, sounds, colors, and textures merge here to create their own world, with the strength and personality of a thousand year old architectural culture.

On the grass, beneath the thick foliage of the trees, two contemporary white chairs in the shape of butterflies invite us to contemplate of this mysterious and magical place.

The water jets at ground level are integrated with the rest of the pool. Under the water, the special treatment applied to the ceramic floor tiles to separate the fountain area from the pool area is clearly evident.

Behind the water fountain, on the carpet of grass, there is a glimpse of the past in the form of an ancient fired clay vessel. The entire pool is surrounded by a thick carpet of grass that comes right up to the edge.

Two drawings that show the landscape architect's original design for the project.

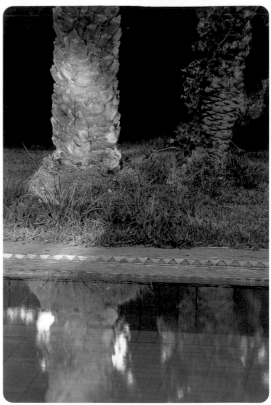

The double edging of fired clay reflects a geometric exercise that is characteristic of this country's tradition.

The stepped entrance invites the visitor to slip into the water and enjoy the beauty of the landscape from an underwater bench.

Inspired by Versailles, this swimming pool imitates the suggestive shapes of the lush gardens at the French royal palace. However, it has a trait all its own: an ingenious system of channels surrounding a small island where six symbolic olive trees grow. There is a continuous movement of water, since this area is connected to a small pool on a lower level. This keeps the swimming pool clean, converts a retaining wall into a charming waterfall, and adds the relaxing sound of running water. At night, an arbor that serves as an informal porch is a magical area for dining, enjoying a final drink, or just chatting.

The pool is perfectly symmetrical, its linearity broken only by two semicircles. The first forms the island and the second, directly across from it, contains underwater steps.

The immensity of the garden has been strictly respected, both on the upper and lower levels. The olive and palm trees, freely spreading their fans of exotic beauty, are the stars of this orchard.

This project integrates the entire respecting the setting. It employs a refined, almost stark style, which brings out the central axis created by the pool, as well as the setting itself, thus creating many perspectives, such as the one framed by the columns of the arbor. Quite an exercise in visual style.

THE ETERNAL CYCLE OF WATER

Location: **Majorca, Spain**
Surface area: **484 sq. ft.**

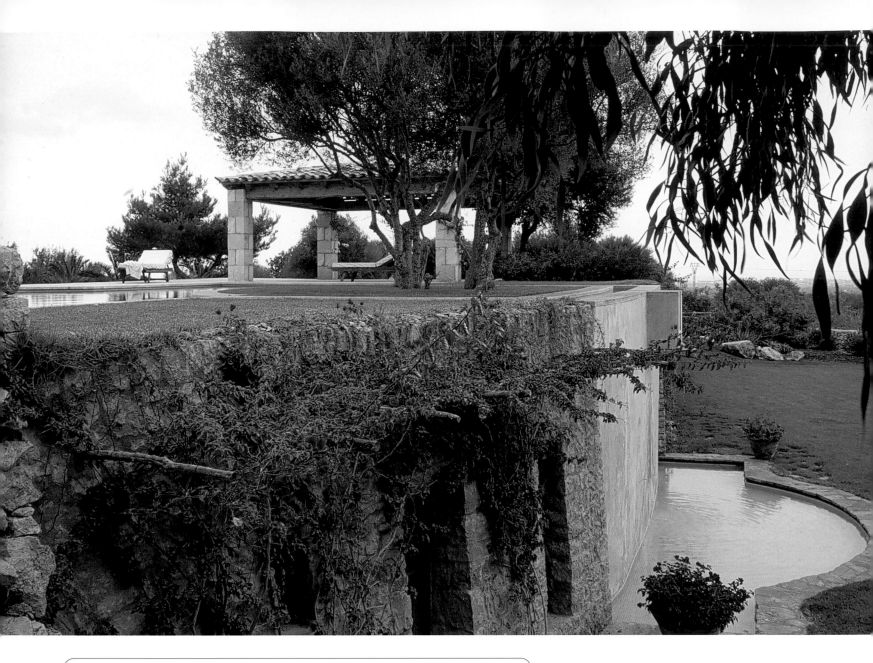

From this angle the two main levels can be seen: the water is the link between them. Bougainvillea dots the immense garden with a variety of warm colors.

The location of the arbor provides a placid, shady area. The pool was shaped using natural slip-proof stone, which was also used for the columns supporting the arbor.

Drawing: the garden and the water area.

Front view of the olive trees, perfectly integrated with the pool and the setting through an ingenious system of channels surrounding this island of vegetation. The visual continuity between the group of trees and the landscape that softly envelops it can be appreciated from any angle.

Five wide steps invite one into the water. Low, natural stone walls delimit the pool and house areas. Right: detail of the rustic shower that emerges from the foliage of an indigenous tree.

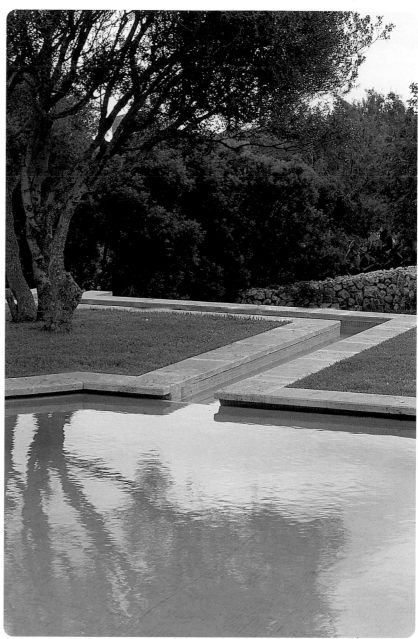

High and low walls mark the different levels as well as the various landscaped areas surrounding the house and pool. A combination of open and more secluded spaces was chosen to enhance enjoyment of the natural beauty.

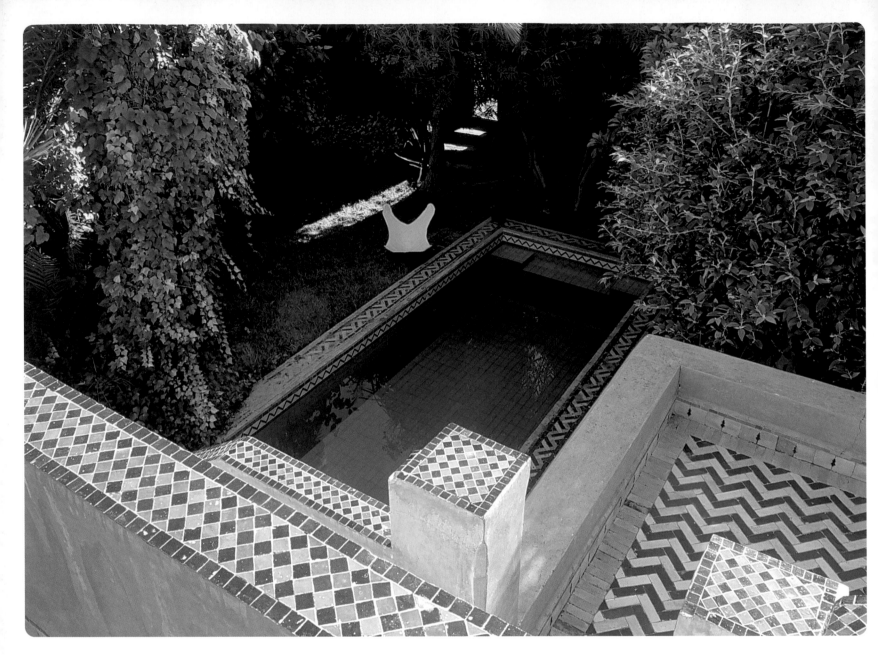

In a magnificent Marrakech palm grove one can make out the unique silhouette of this house, protected by a high sand-colored wall which, among other things, shields the landscaped area and main building from the harshness of the sun. Inside, levels and gradients extend from the one central point, the interior patio, as is the custom in this culture.

Starting from this visual center, the architectural rhythm of the house and exterior areas is presented as a series of discontinuous spaces that create amazing perspectives which can be enjoyed from anywhere in the house.

The pool area is surrounded by a multicolored garden where palm trees, yuccas, climbers, fragrant plants, and various fruit trees are responsible for the special microclimate of this space, which is much cooler than the outside during the summer. A soft carpet of grass covers the garden right up to the pool's edge.

On the opposite side, a green mosaic covers the strip between the pool and the garden wall, unifying all the colors on the ground. A restrained geometric border in elegant tones, the only note of color in this decidedly herbaceous setting, decorates the upper edges and the top of the inner perimeter.

IN THE SHADE OF A
PALM GROVE

Location: **Douar Abiat, Marrakech**
Surface area: **108 sq. ft.**

A restrained geometric border in elegant tones, the only note of color in this setting, decorates the upper edges of the pool and the top of the inner perimeter.

The pool is surrounded by a garden that features a wide range of indigenous vegetation. The garden creates its own microclimate that protects it from the heat.

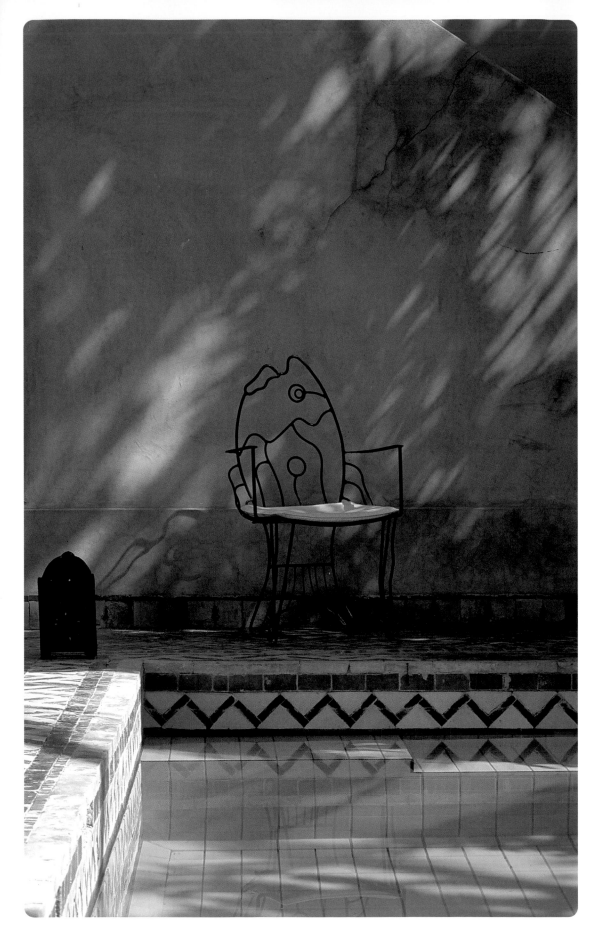

A stylized iron chair in the shape of a fish casts its shadow on the façade, which is sand-colored, like the inside of the pool.

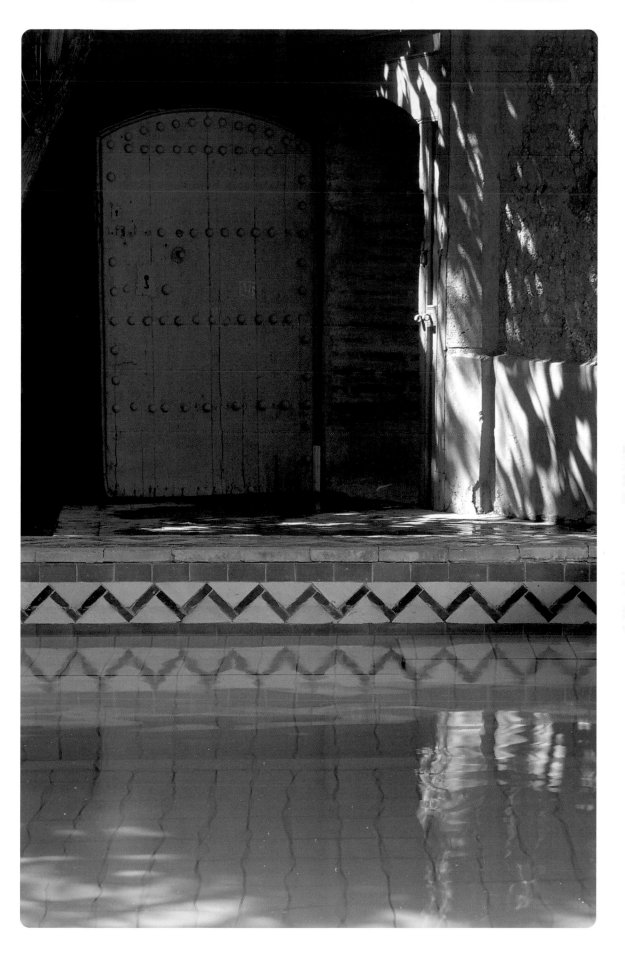

A typical Moroccan wooden door, studded and painted in a soft turquoise, connects the main building with the recreation area.

With elegant simplicity, this unique pool seems to capture the passage of time, which is almost halted in this space dedicated to contemplation and beauty and carved in every stone. Two levels of water are enhanced by an elaborate exercise in gardening which softens the chromatic melancholy of the stone, faded and polished by the indelible mark of man and time.

Surrounded by a delicate iron railing, which sometimes disappears amid the vegetation, this water area is comprised of two surfaces on different levels connected by a stone channel. The upper level, an ancient reservoir, is connected by an old system of water channels to the lower level, which is actually the main pool.

A magnificent pergola bordered by thick hedges marks the center of this symbolic composition and visually delimits the two spaces. In the middle, as if spouting from the earth itself, a peaceful jet of water murmurs tirelessly inside a perfect circle of stone located exactly mid-way between the two levels. With the singular familiarity of a sundial, the fountain marks the geometry of the pergola, which surrounds and protects it.

To strengthen the composition, the ground was completely paved with cobblestones of varying shades of gray that sparkle only when caressed by the sun.

CARVED

IN STONE

Location: **Mollégés, France**
Surface area: **322 sq. ft.**

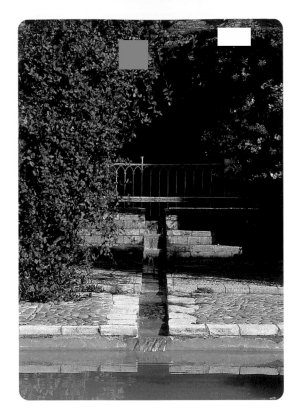

Detail of the central fountain that joins the two levels. The entire area was paved with cobblestones of varying shades of gray.

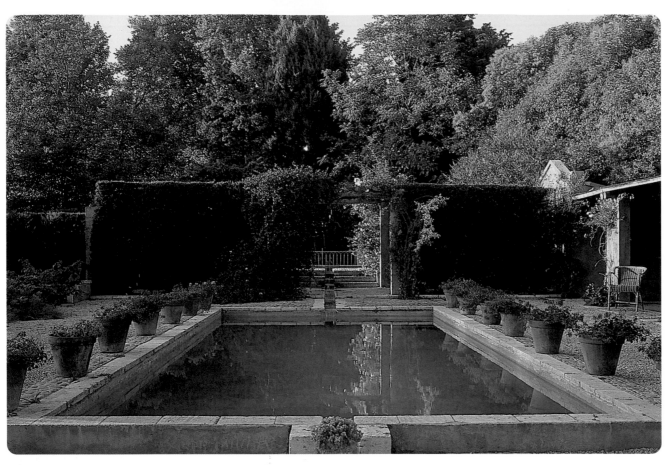

Wide view of the main pool, enclosed by a solid border of rustic stone with two symmetrical rows of clay flowerpots filled with cheerful red geraniums.

A view of the main pool's outlet, where a disordered pile of river rocks acts as a natural filter, blocking leaves and other impurities.

This semi-overflowing swimming pool, surrounded and protected by a luxuriant forest of Mediterranean pine, is situated at a level below the house, or principal structure. Connected by a simple path of natural stone, the presence of the water is announced as a sudden explosion among the dry, fragrant pines.

At the end of the path, a broad, smooth slope reminiscent of typical Mediterranean fishing wharves is an invitation to plunge into the coolness of the turquoise water. The lively tonality was achieved by coating the inside of the pool in a light tone — a simple way to achieve bright, colorful effects by means of the contrast with the natural greens.

Crowned with a broad edging of cream-colored artificial stone, the perimeter of the pool combines lines and soft curves, creating a totally balanced volume, in contrast to the architectural hardness of the house. The irregular shape of the pool, the elevation of the land, and the line of overflowing water not only lend personality and character to this composition, but also offer interesting visual perspectives, since the pool is at treetop level.

The overflow area was created in response to both aesthetic and functional concerns: this system makes it easy to maintain the pool because the water's movement clears away the needles of the surrounding pines.

Almost at the level of the water, the slender figures of weather-beaten tree trunks frame the entrance to the pool, standing like symbolic, welcoming bulrushes.

THE COLOR TURQUOISE

Location: **Ibiza, Spain**
Surface area: **408 sq. ft.**

74

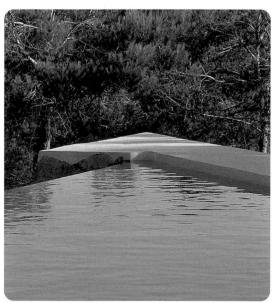

The pool lies, peaceful and filled with color, below the house. Its balanced volume was created to contrast with the house's architectural hardness. In the photo on the left, the ramp inspired by typical Mediterranean fishing wharves can be seen.

Detail of the line of overflowing water, which blends the pool with the pines that surround and protect it. On a second level, the horizon line and the blue color of the sea.

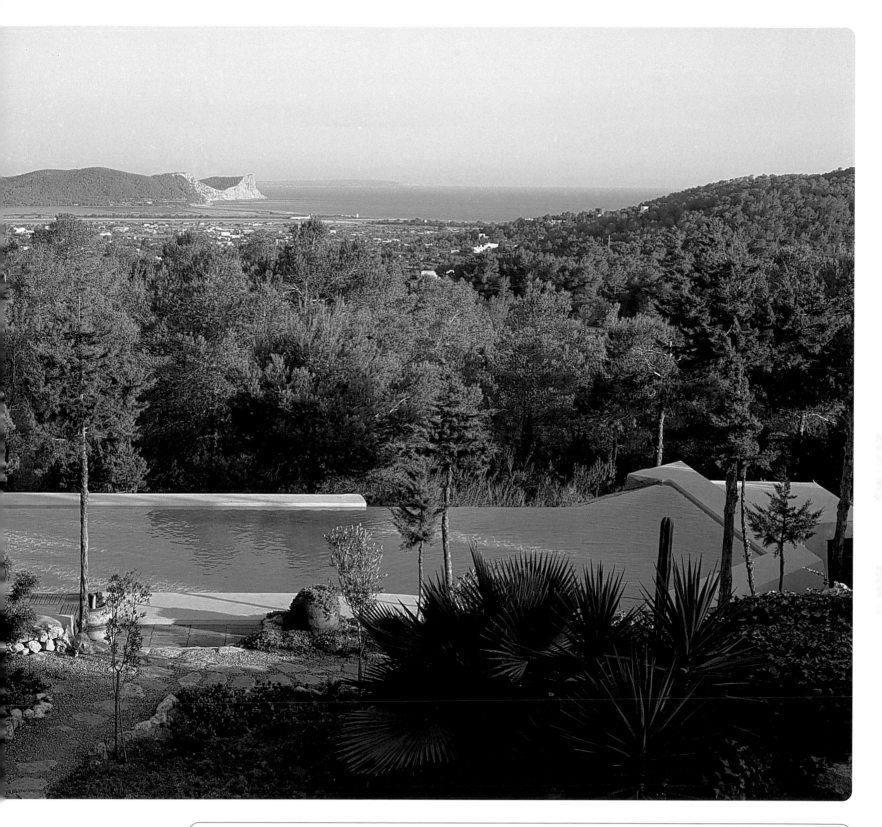

The location of the swimming pool, below the house and surrounded by a dense pine forest, affords isolation, intimacy, and protection.

This splendid garden, which extends generously to the east and west of the property, was conceived as a succession of individual spaces, chromatically differentiated but united by an imaginary straight line. On one side, this line takes the form of a watercourse, and on the other, it blends with the green hues of the grass that carpets the entrance to the rear gardens.

Four classical gardens extend from the unique central point of the magnificent restored house, painted a vanilla color. Two of them include conceptually different pools: one for visual amusement, and the other for swimming. The studied landscaping invites reflection while it sparks the stroller's secret internal creativity with the rapid succession of different spaces, lovingly landscaped and united by organically vivid optical effects and visual perspectives.

The area opposite the porch, previously the site of a metal sheep shed, now contains a serene pond which reflects the warm light of French Provence and the shadow of a stand of unyielding plane trees. A series of massive balls, carved out of solid rock, the eternal symbol of perfection, align themselves with balanced precision on ancient bases in front of the pond.

Another highlight is the stylized Aeolian fountain, also in the form of a circle of vegetation, from which crystalline water flows as a soft breeze blows. Fish, ducks, and frogs inhabit this water area, which is covered by water lilies in velvet tones. A water channel flows from the pond, and extends between a long line of olive and cypress trees, terminating some 262 feet later in a small pool shaped like a half moon, surrounded by iris and willows.

CLASSICAL SPIRIT

Location: Saint-Rémy de Provence, France
Surface area: **129 sq. ft.**

The silhouettes of the plane trees, chosen to provide shade, are reflected in the pond, opposite the porch.

Although conceived as individual elements of a sequence, the spaces are united by a straight waterway edged by a long line of olive and cypress trees.

One color, white jade, and a single material, a clay-like stone from a quarry, are the two key elements that serve as

MINIMALIST CHARACTER

a thread between the main building and the water area to produce a homogeneous architectural volume. In fact, starting from one of the side walls that shelter the house's winter porch, the pool becomes the logical extension of the house.

To accentuate the integration of both spaces, the pool was structured on two levels that merge into one: the level that starts at the winter porch, where three large windows shaped like sliding doors open up, and another that starts at the summer porch, where the stairs to the pool are located. Thus, the water does not just surround the interior and exterior recreation areas, but is also a calm, restrained, modern pool with a highly refined style.

The ubiquitous white stone, which surrounds the property like a protective cloak, embellishes the house,

and adds an element of surprise due to its unique clay-like texture and smooth luminosity, which highlight the linearity of the grouping and add a certain formal dynamism. In keeping with this approach, the summer porch was paved with the same material, so the pool is connected with this exterior area. A thin netting, manipulated by means of a sophisticated mechanism, serves as a minimalist canopy in an area intended basically for sunbathing during the day and as a summer porch at night.

As for the garden, its elegant, green carpet of grass brings out the luminosity of the stone. At the main entrance to the house, a pine tree more than 50 years old welcomes visitors and is the only vertical element in a garden that prefers to spotlight the architectural work.

Location: **Miami, Fl., USA**
Surface area: **150 sq. ft.**

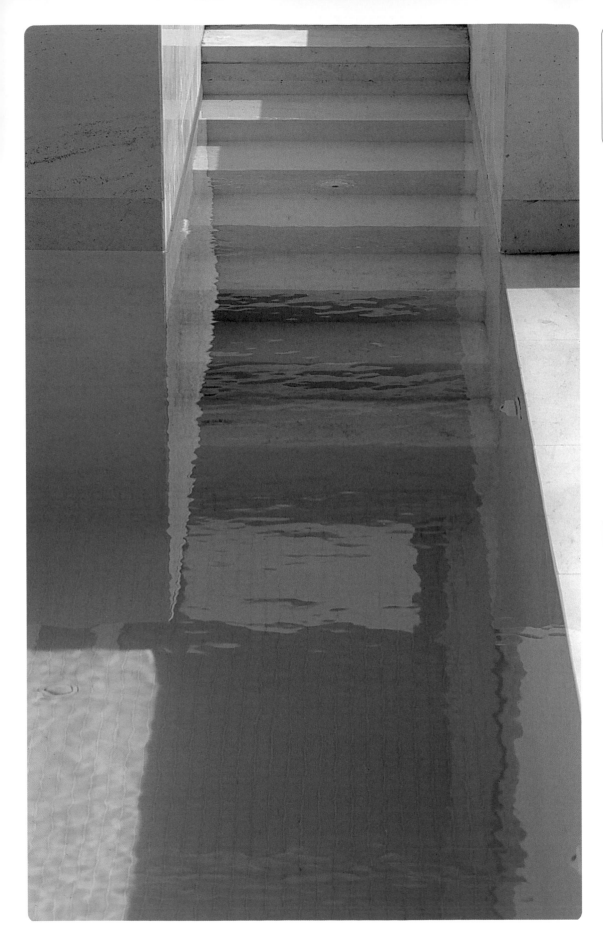

Opposite the luminous summer porch is the entrance to the pool, a narrow stairway between two wide, low walls that function as a solid banister. The pool was built of the same clay-like material used for the house. It comes from a quarry.

Detail of the horizontal opening that provides light to the underground garage. At the back, the water glides over the low wall in a flat cascade.

Refined, almost monastic, this swimming pool recaptures the identity of the Roman thermae, the ancient public baths known for their importance as social centers. But here the aesthetic of Roman civilization has been replaced by an austere, restrained style that comes to life only with the caress of sunlight.

PRIVATE SPACE

Built as an independent structure attached to the main dwelling, the pool is sheltered from the wind by three high, intensely white walls. The types of palm and pines trees surrounding the house peek over the walls. The pool's rectangular shape occupies almost the entire space, leaving just a narrow strip that functions as both ornamental trim and walkway.

The continuity of the white color enhances the formal balance of the composition. The chromatic contrast is accentuated through the use of the color indigo, the client's requirement, to coat the pool's interior. Throughout the day, the play of light and shadow imparts volume and geometry to the grouping. At nightfall, the heat accumulated during the daylight hours keeps the water warm.

In addition to providing physical pleasure, this unique pool is also an intimate, private space, ideal for meditation.

Location: **Ibiza, Spain**
Surface area: **54 sq. ft.**

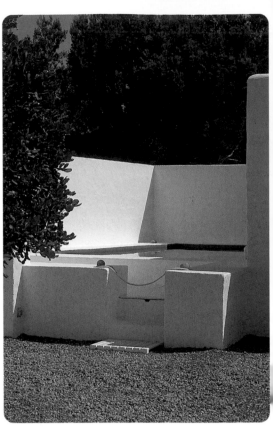

The work's linearity offers bright, colorful geometric perspectives, such as the one that can be enjoyed from the entrance. A narrow strip of blue color frames the water, giving it visual depth.

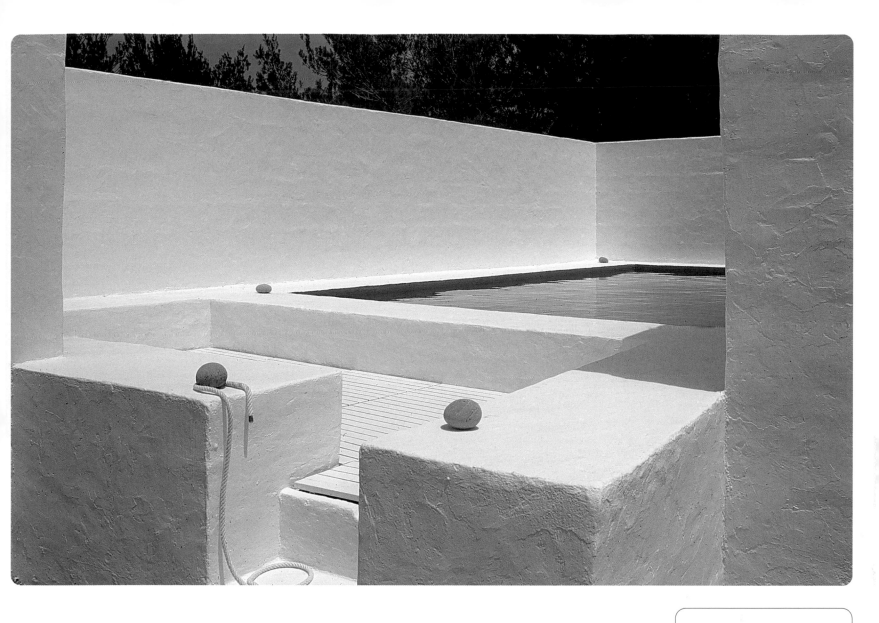

Access is by two built-in steps. Levels and gradients are geometrically balanced by the continuity of the white color.

Beyond the twisted trunk of an old carob tree, the different levels of the pool are visible. The key to its formal balance lies in the restrained style and two-color chromaticity.

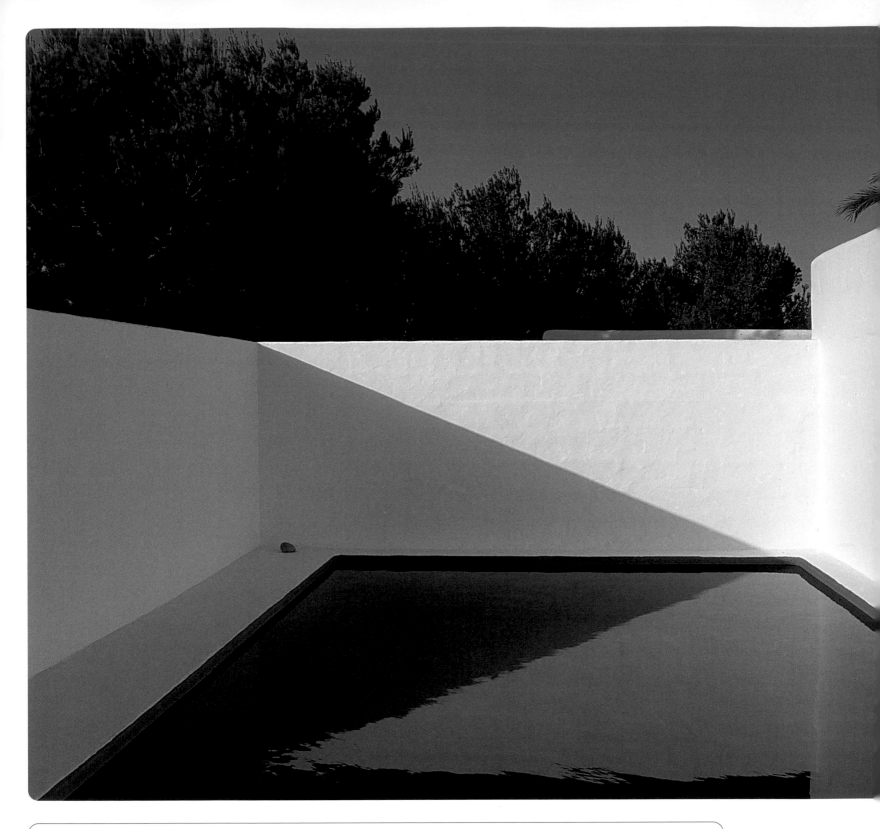

Three tall walls painted in an intense white color shelter the pool from the wind. The tops of the pine and palm trees that surround the house peek over the wall.

Throughout the day, the light creates different shadows that impart volume and geometry to this chromatically contrasted space.

On the edge of a small thicket-forest, this pool, in the shape of a Hispano-Arab irrigation channel, emerges like a placid mountain river. The quiet murmur of a fountain, placed strategically between two rows of stairs leading to the water, completes this balanced, mature landscape whose reminders of the past fade as one studies the grouping as a whole.

The visual center of this project is the low sculptured wall that encloses the pool and also provides a means of entering the water. In addition to optically isolating the pool from the more wooded area of the garden, its texture and chromatic streaks, together with the flat fountain between the two areas, consti-

tute an original way to formally balance a narrow, long pool.

This visual expedient, together with the studied landscaping, has softened the pool's excessive linearity. In fact, just a glance away from the center of attention are two soft patches of grass serenely surrounding the pool, countering its formal hardness. The different tones of the nearby vegetation and the colorful presence of a magnificent bougainvillea, which covers the porch of the house, are the elements that visually order the natural setting, making it a self-contained, easily-maintained garden.

INSPIRED BY THE PAST

Location: **Majorca, Spain**
Surface area: **408 sq. ft.**

The linearity of this pool, shaped like an irrigation channel, is softened by two grassy slopes covered with easily-maintained vegetation. As the only note of color, a magnificent bougainvillea graces the porch adjacent to the pool.

Melting into the immense horizon on this island is not just a privilege, but a singular tribute to the natural beauty.

THE MAGIC OF A SETTING

Location: **Ibiza, Spain**
Surface area: **322 sq. ft.**

Through the use of carefully-placed gradients, a linear geometry that creates spectacular perspectives, and a palette based on just one color, blue, a magnificent composition has been achieved that extends visually to the depths of the sea and sky.

One of the keys to the grouping is the exterior profile of the swimming pool, which simulates being on a level with the sea. To enhance this effect, the interior of the pool has been coated white, increasing the contrast of tones while creating a white geometric border, like an optical interlude between the intense blue of the sea and the crystalline hues of the pool water.

The simple lines of the two porches, combined with the use of unusual materials such as cement, which crowns the pool and covers its entire perimeter, and iron, which acts as the principal support of the exterior structure, are the key elements to its integration with the surroundings. Actually, the use of these two construction materials makes it possible to play with new textures while they concede the starring role to the majesty of the landscape and add character to this unique grouping.

The decoration has followed the same principle: intelligent design and innovative materials for outdoor furniture with a distinctive style.

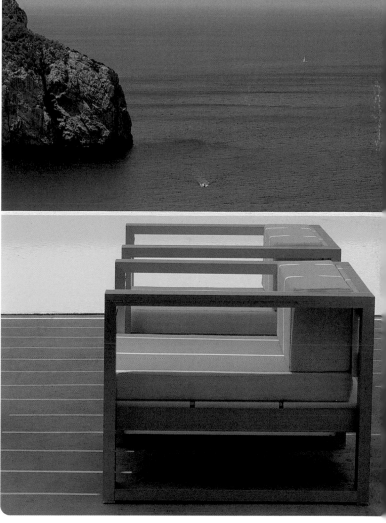

Innovative materials and furnishings with a contemporary style were chosen for the exterior decoration.

At dusk, the colors blend and the textures soften. The grouping takes on an aura of serenity in perfect harmony with the setting, but always concedes the starring role to the beauty of the landscape.

Changing with the light, the color of the pool water merges with the sea. The different textures of the water, in constant motion, create moments of incredible beauty, as if it were a spectacular kaleidoscope.

This original water area is situated in an old restored Mexican ranch and framed by multiple visual perspectives. Located on the house's uncovered patio, it was conceived as a small, cistern-like pool, inspired by old-fashioned washhouses. Symmetrically aligned, six jets circulate the water and create a smooth, natural melody that can be heard from any corner.

In this project, space, color, and the texture of a single material, concrete, merge and complement each other to create a setting rich in nuances, where the light participates directly in creating volumes and perspective. In fact, the forcefulness of the color serves a dual purpose here: to soften the sober quality of the area and to visually lower the height of the room, creating a cool place of refuge from the summer heat. An intense earth color, a warm orangish tone that stands out in clear contrast, was chosen for the floor.

For decoration, both the furnishings and ornamental elements were carefully chosen to serve as sculptures in a unique artistic exercise. A collection of little bronze statues at strategic locations around the pool, a painting subtly placed on one of the ends, the old swinging bench on the upper level, or even the group of ferns as the only plant life, acquire a special prominence enhanced by the presence of color. Finally, a delicate white dove crowns this beautiful composition, a symbol of peace that, in and of itself, conveys the character of this room.

CHROMATIC PERSONALITY

Location: **Jalisco, Mexico**
Surface area: **120 sq. ft.**

An etched glass door separates the water area, located on the semi-covered central patio, from the luminous interior of the house. The chromatic contrasts and informal balance can be appreciated from the threshold of the entryway.

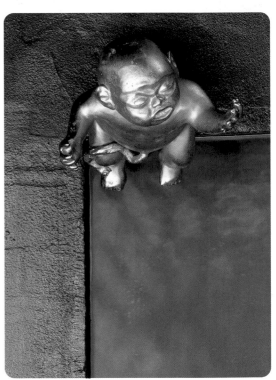

The pool, an intense indigo blue, was constructed with concrete, the same material that covers the floor, which is painted in earth tones and has the advantage of being easy to maintain and water-resistant since this patio area is semi-covered.

Symmetrically aligned, six slender jets circulate the water in the pool, creating a domesticated but bright and colorful cascade, which can be heard almost anywhere in the house.

Peeking out from a small, steep cove, the exceptional location of this pool captures all the beauty of the landscape,

VANTAGE POINT

which extends toward infinity. Its irregular, wedge-shaped perimeter, with soft, unusual curves, stops at the edge of the cliff, and accommodates three different levels. At the sharpest bend, a first step facilitates entry into the pool. A second skirts the side and forms a kind of underwater bench for relaxing, and the deepest part is at yet a third level.

A single material was used inside the pool and the area surrounding it: lime cement, with a typically Mediterranean texture and tonality. Also typically Mediterranean are the pines, which provide the only note of color in this universe of dazzling luminosity.

The design of this pool, built without ornamental trim but with rounded edges, is more about aesthetics and leisure than swimming. Admiring the scenery is paramount, albeit comfortably settled in the water.

This beautiful and powerful landscape is in constant motion, subject to the will of the light. The pool becomes a unique, serene vantage point from which to contemplate, at any time of day, the play and subtle changes of light. By any standard, a privilege.

Location: **Santorini, Greece**
Surface area: **130 sq. ft.**

The pool's exceptional location makes it possible to enjoy the sunsets from a unique vantage point.

The pines provide a note of color in this composition dominated by white and blue.

The immensity of the sea and the infinity of the landscape can be enjoyed from any of the pool's three levels.

This unique overflowing pool is hidden away in the rocky wall of an old quarry high on a hill. To obtain the perfect fusion of the construction project and the natural setting, a natural recess in the rocky wall was used. The result is spectacular: an imposing wall of rock, eroded on one side by water from an artificial waterfall and covered on the other side by a blanket of plant life that softens the roughness of the stone.

The pool was treated like a sheet of water, although it resembles the small, deep, natural rock ponds in the eastern part of the Alps, where the water stays frozen even at the height of summer. The rocky wall was kept practically intact, even the submerged area, respecting its formal structure and unmistakable texture. The main entrance reveals, in detail, the merging of the rocky wall with the volume of the pool.

Levels and gradients structure the placement of two extensive terraces paved with fired clay flagstones whose reddish color adds a note of warmth while highlighting the contrast with the light color of the rock. The simplicity of the natural materials enhances the rustic effect of the grouping, although it is softened by the sophisticated iron sun loungers and the elegant color of the upholstered cushions.

IN THE HEART OF A QUARRY

Location: **Barcelona, Spain**
Surface area: **215 sq. ft.**

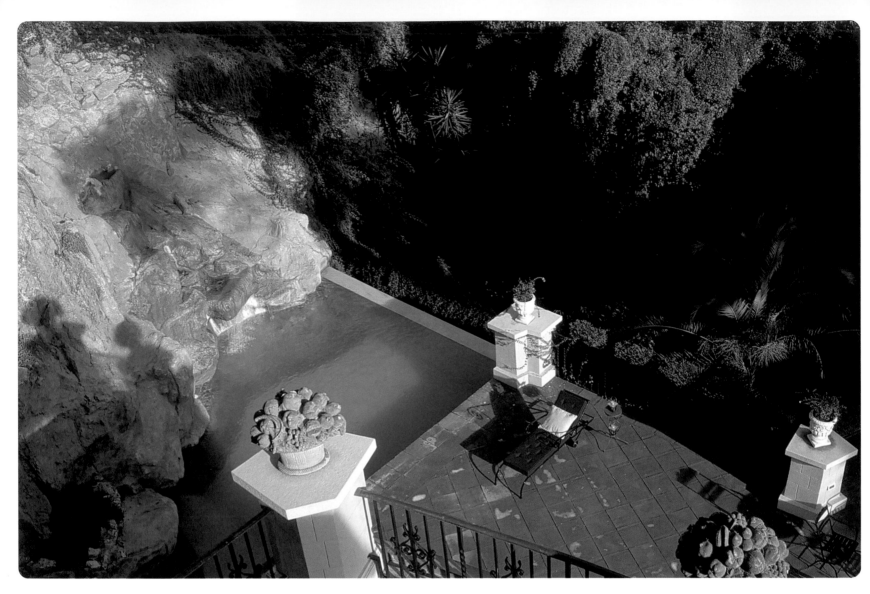

Spectacular view of the pool and lower terrace. The shape of the old stone quarry, now a luxuriant garden, can still be seen amid the thick vegetation.

123

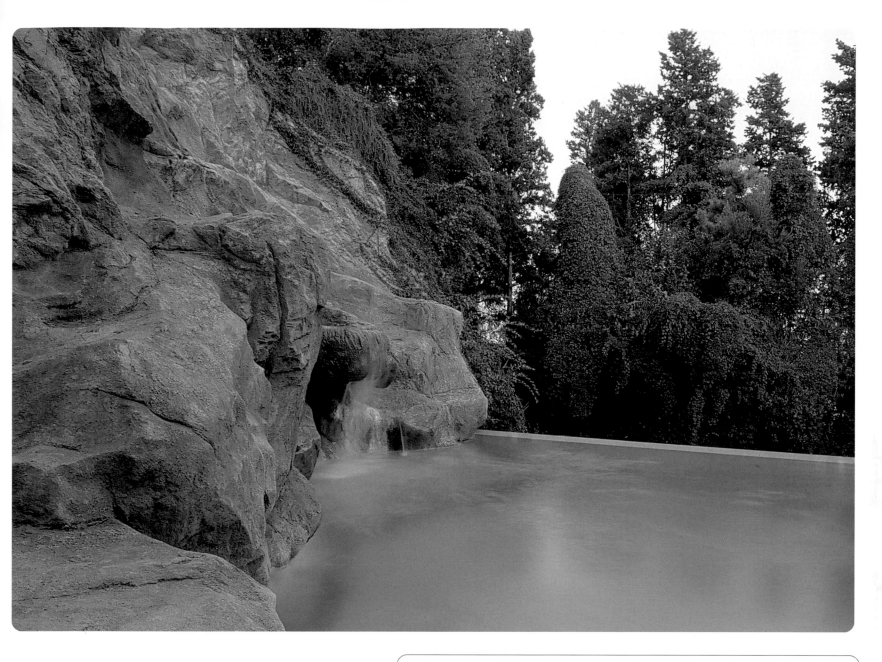

The pool was treated like a sheet of water, although it resembles the small, deep, natural rock ponds where the water stays frozen even at the height of summer.

The rocky wall was kept practically intact, even the submerged area, respecting its formal structure and unmistakable texture. The merging of the rocky wall with the volume of the pool can be seen in detail at the main entrance.

This serene pool rests in a deck of tropical wood which comes flush up against the rear façade of the house. The highly-stylized, formally-refined project, in which the pool is on the same level as the thick carpet of grass which covers the entire garden, was built on a highly-contrasted chromatic base of three intense colors – organic green, deep blue, and honey brown.

Constructed with Mediterranean-blue gresite and finished inside with the same wood that covers the area, the pool has an entrance which is visually separated from the composition to break the pool's rectangular line. The tropical wood deck that shelters the water and covers the entire outdoor lounging area imparts a sensation of visual dynamism and a touch of velvety warmth.

To unify materials and textures, the dividing wall between properties was designed with the same tropical wood used for the deck and the roof of the minimalist pavilion, which was built as an outdoor lounge. For this more protected and intimate space, stylized sofas and a central table made of iron were chosen, as well as tropical wood sun loungers in a slightly more rustic style.

A thin steel rail visually unites the grouping with the interior bay window at the corner of the house and separates the outside lounging area from the façade.

ZEN SYMMETRY

Location: **Barcelona, Spain**
Surface area: **270 sq. ft.**

Wide view of the pool and outdoor lounging area, which is sheltered by a minimalist pavilion. The tropical wood gives the setting a touch of visual dynamism and integrates the pool and lounging area on a single level.

For this project, the typical edging was rejected in order to visually integrate the pool area with the tropical wood deck. From this angle, one can see the solution to the problem of the interior finish of the pool's edge.

This magnificent trapezoidal pool is surrounded by a spectacular deck of tonka bean tree wood. Situated next to the main building — a country house — this area was designed and visually linked to the adjacent building with the unifying element of a tropical deck wood, colored an intense brown.

The restoration of the country house, the construction of the pool, and the reclamation of the secondary building as a water area, occurred slowly and in stages over a period of more than five years. To be precise, the entire water area was planned in a last phase, when the owners bought the adjacent property, which now houses a complete leisure area with Finnish sauna, Turkish bath, and changing rooms situated under an impressive arch which reaches up to the ceiling of the old building. A jacuzzi, strategically placed to take advantage of views of the Ampurdan landscape, completes this formally balanced, oversized room whose refined style harmonizes different textures: stone, etched glass, and tropical wood.

Outside, a wall of varying heights, perfectly restored and crowned with a bright, colorful tapestry of vegetation, isolates and protects the area and creates an intimate, cozy space. Moreover, the intelligent combination of colors and textures, including the green of the vegetation, the pale ochre of the stone, and the chromatic intensity of the tonka bean tree wood deck, enhances a blended set of natural contrasts that make the grouping a splendid exercise in integrating landscape and architecture

EXERCISE IN CONTRASTS

Location: **Girona, Spain**
Surface area: **484 sq. ft.**

A wall of varying heights, in conjunction with a dense, colorful layer of vegetation, affords an intimate and cozy space.

Tonka bean tree wood was chosen for its great chromatic intensity to cover the water area. The wood enhances the blended set of contrasts.

The beautiful Ampurdan landscape can be enjoyed from the jacuzzi.

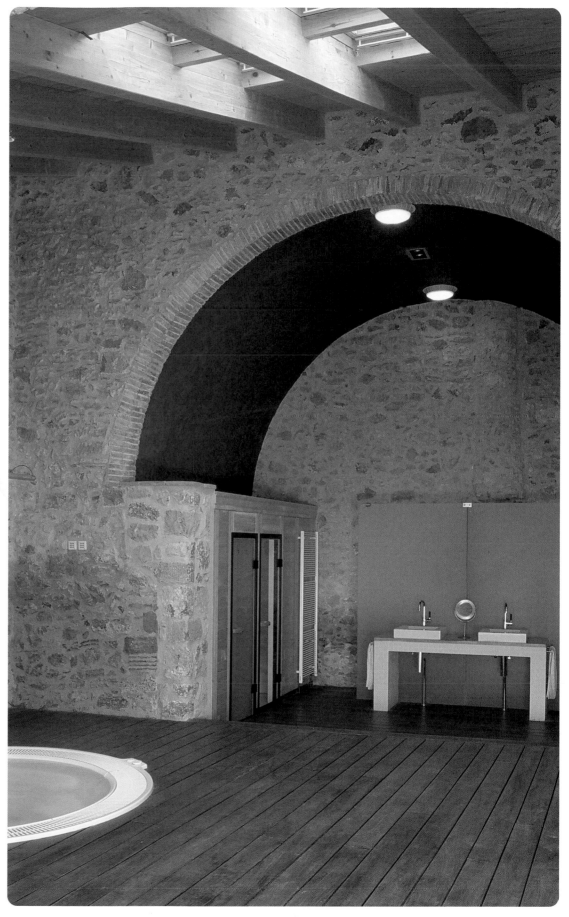

A sauna and Turkish bath are situated under an impressive arch which reaches up to the ceiling of the existing building.

137

The passage of the years has left its patina on this complex landscape composition, to which the pool is a worthy addition. The presence of many ponds, parterres, and beautifully paved paths that lead us unhurriedly to the different areas of the garden, make the pool a secondary but perfectly integrated element of this kaleidoscope of plant life.

Surrounding the pool area are several pavilions, whitewashed and coated with a layer of lime mortar. These small structures provide the only note of color in a composition featuring earth tones and an extensive fan of greens. Amid the columns, custom-made benches provide a place to chat in the shade. The inside of the pool, also whitewashed, enhances the continuity of the materials and the colors of the setting.

The surrounding area is organized around a low garden that includes papyrus, which grows in the ponds, and cyca, a very slow-growing Japanese species. The plants are combined with various trees, including ancient olives, which symbolically preside over the entrance to the pool area. In this composition, the vegetation has been sculpted, modeled, and dominated by the hand of man, transformed according to his concept of beauty.

Located on an upper level, separated from the garden by a dividing wall, is an orchard of fruit trees on a carpet of grass. The distribution of the different garden areas, the constant presence of water, and the serene meandering of the paths, were inspired by cloister orchards and gardens.

The patina of time

Location: **Ibiza, Spain**
Surface area: **516 sq. ft.**

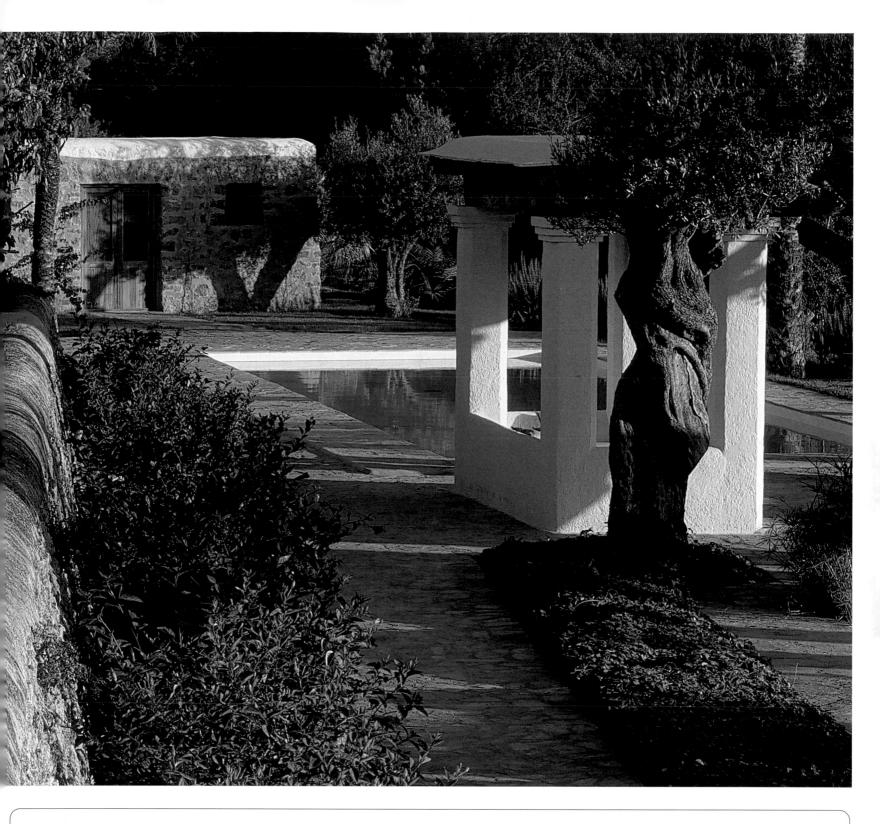

On a level above the pool, set apart by a low dividing wall, is a row of vines that lead to an orchard of fruit trees. At the back, a restored stone hut coated with a layer of lime mortar houses the garden tools.

The cloister's orchards and gardens inspired the constant presence of water and the serene appearance of the paths.

Two plant species are prominent in this garden setting: papyrus, which grows in the ponds, and cyca, a very slow-growing species.

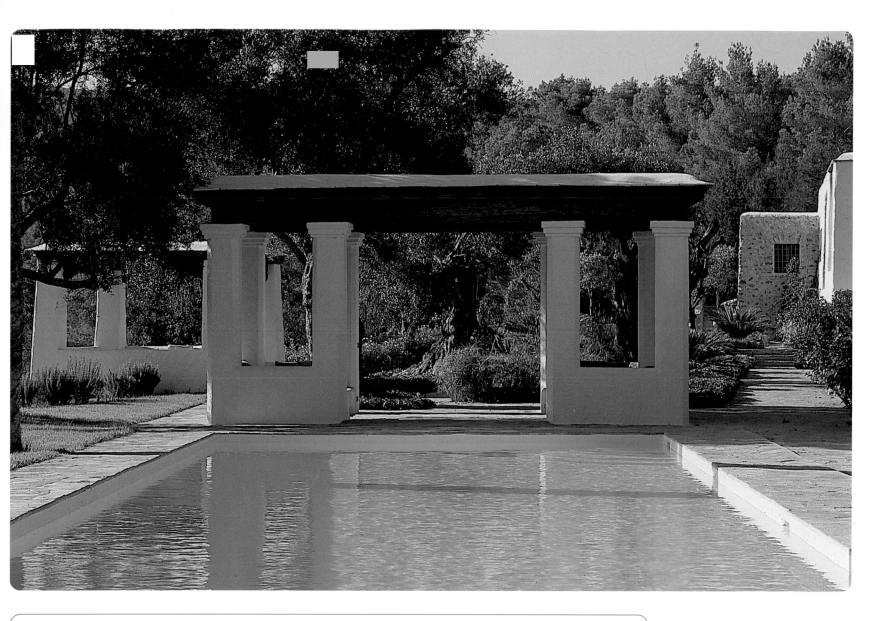

The columns of this pavilion, with custom-made benches where one can enjoy the shade, frame the pool and afford a beautiful view.

The well is still used by the owners of the house.

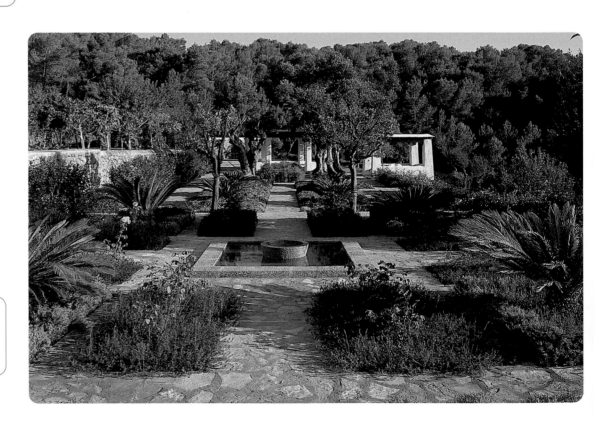

A square fountain is the visual center where the garden and main path begin. The path leads to the water and to the pavilion.

This pool's layout follows the model of the classical houses of French Provence, with two clearly differentiated exterior spaces. Situated opposite the house's rear façade, directly in front of the main rooms to facilitate direct access, this delicious water area is well-defined and clearly organized, starting with the various hedges that stretch out in succession from the façade.

On one level is the pool, peaceful, welcoming and classic, with the subtle elegance that only the passage of time and the hand of an expert gardener can achieve. Formally, it is finished with a rustic crown of natural stone, and the inside is coated with blue gresite. Large slabs of unglazed, fired clay pave this recreational area, adding a warm chromatic note and ensuring easy maintenance year round.

This pool's enchanting character is mainly a result of the deliberate, studied French-style landscaping. The garden, conceived as a natural extension of the house, maintains a delicate symmetry of plant life. Boxwood hedges of different heights visually separate the various landscaped areas. A hammock, the only informal element in this composition, hangs from a refined, stylized, solid wooden structure, which also supports a thick, climbing rose bush, making it the focal point of the grouping.

Opposite the house, in the landscaped area, sits a small, ancient stone cistern for collecting rainwater. The presence of this beautiful cistern confirms the personality and style of the property.

CLASSICAL

PERSONALITY

Location: **Les Beaux de Provence, France**
Surface area: **344 sq. ft.**

146

The pool can be accessed from the main rooms of the house through quaint landscaped parterres that form a path parallel to the rear façade.

Opposite the main entrance, a beautiful, ancient solid stone water fountain sits next to a small cistern for collecting rainwater.

This spectacular project started from a few ruins, now formally integrated into the pool. The recovery and reinterpretation of ancient construction systems is an outgrowth of the traditional habitat, based on one material, earth, and one process, adobe, which involves building with bricks made of earth mixed with straw and dried in the sun.

Used by man for approximately 10,000 years to build houses and cities, this material is enjoying a strong resurgence because it is environmentally friendly and insulating, keeping the structure cool in summer and warm in winter in a totally natural manner. Nevertheless, the recovery of this earth architecture stems not just from the interest in the tradition, but also from the very modern concern for the ecology.

For this project, located in a Moroccan paradise – the Marrakech palm grove – a group of ancient ruins was converted into an evocative sculpture, perfectly integrated with the setting and the pool.

The walls were restored with adobe brick, then covered by hand with unbaked adobe, and finally coated with plant oils for protection and preservation.

A pavilion in a restrained style presides over the pool, chromatically united with the grouping through an intense ochre, the color of earth, which is also present in the coating of the dividing walls.

THE VALUE OF THE PAST

Location: **Marrakech, Morocco**
Surface area: **485 sq. ft.**

Wide view of the pool, showing the unique overflowing effect. This pool is based on a series of discontinuous levels centered on a group of ancient ruins, now restored and integrated into the project by architect Charles Boccara.

Detail of the sophisticated ornamentation decorating the base of the pool entrance. The walls are covered with adobe applied by hand and coated with plant oils for protection and preservation.

A pavilion in a restrained style presides over the pool, chromatically united with the grouping through an intense ochre, the color of earth.

On the page to the right a look at the special texture of the hand-applied adobe, which produces the effect of being superimposed.

Despite its apparent symmetry, this project on the island of Majorca is in keeping with the criteria of oriental architecture, based on discontinuity, broken lines, and the lack of a single focal point.

Flanked by majestic palm trees is a swimming pool whose edges are elegantly submerged in the water. To the right and on the same level as the still surface of the water, a small square building with a vaulted roof, fronted by a refined, rectilinear porch, rises up like a burst of color. It is an amazing hamam, whose interior, in the shape of an octagonal star, follows the guidelines of Arab symbolic geometry. Two colors, purplish-blue and soft ochre, dominate the room and filter the exterior luminosity, inviting one to remain under its intimate protection.

Opposite, a second structure demands attention: erected with strong posts, a large jaima, or traditional Berber tent, in the purest Arab style. Also situated on the same level as the water, its imposing presence is accompanied by a new element, the dry sound of the wind whipping the fabric.

Exotic shapes and uncommon textures are combined in this unique project, where space and architectonic rhythm acquire a multiple dimension based on the most subtle emotions and senses.

NOMADIC SENSATIONS

Location: **Majorca, Spain**
Surface area: **483 sq. ft.**

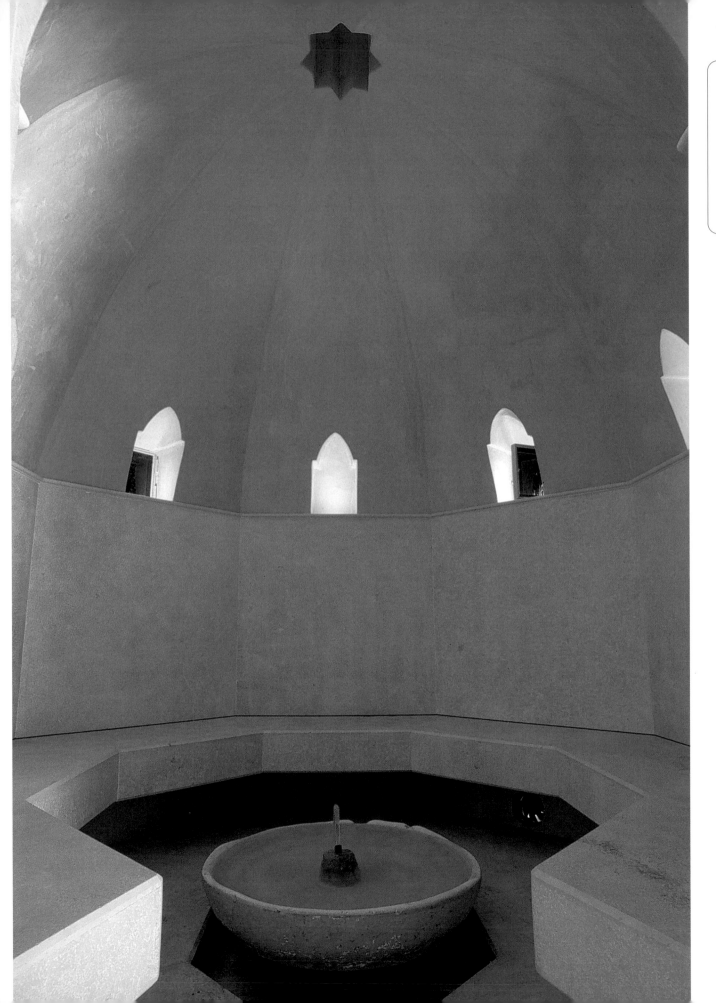

Despite its square exterior shape, the interior of this amazing hamam follows the guidelines of Arab symbolic geometry and is shaped like an octagonal star. Water as a source of life and wealth is the great central character of this unique, oriental-style project..

The presence of a hama with harmonic proportions, fixed with solid posts reaching down to the water, introduces a new element: the sound of the wind hitting the fabric.

Side view of the porch and façade. The magnificent, soft ochre hamam is hidden behind.

Detail of the underwater steps. The exceptionally wide stairway and steps, in combination with the slightly sloped, submerged edge, provide a touch of restrained elegance. The color of the outer perimeter was selected to blend with the ochre tones of the hamam's walls.

This hamam is sophisticated, but follows the traditional patterns. A continuous, balanced series of arches defines the different spaces, chromatically united by one color, a soft ochre, and one material, marble, used on the floor and in the tall baseboards. Nooks and crannies structure different sitting areas, as required by the rules of the hamam, and make it possible to enjoy the art of conversation with a certain discretion and intimacy.

Finishing off the marble baseboard, a stylized geometrical border in tricolored ceramic breaks up the chromatic homogeneity, filtered by indirect light from the transoms, skylights, and windows in the different rooms. The communal water area is square in design, with benches submerged in the cold water. In the dif-

ferent rooms of the hamam, the wood and brass receptacles, which contain cold water to refresh the user, are the only objects that have not been built into the space, due to the need to replace the water regularly.

Finally, and as required by tradition, one can savor a delicious mint tea and enjoy a few minutes of peace in the sitting room adjacent to the hamam, with views of a magnificent enclosed garden. In this room, the ceiling is lined with laurel wood previously colored with natural pigments, handcrafted using an ancient pre-Saharan technique, and the floor is covered with traditional Moroccan decorative shapes and colors.

SENSORIAL SPACE

Location: **Douar Abiat, Morocco**
Surface area: **100 sq. ft.**

164

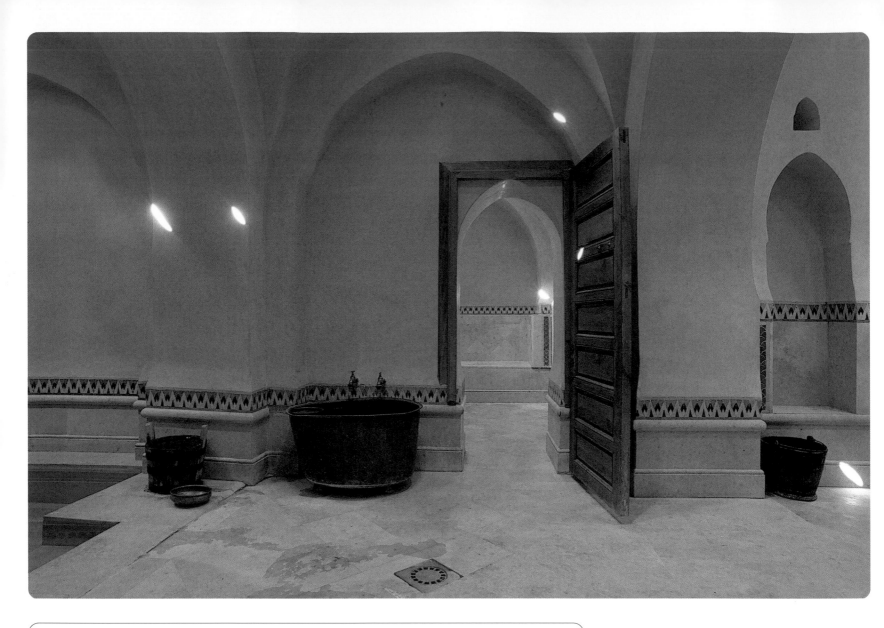

A continuous, balanced series of arches defines the different spaces, finished in a soft ochre.

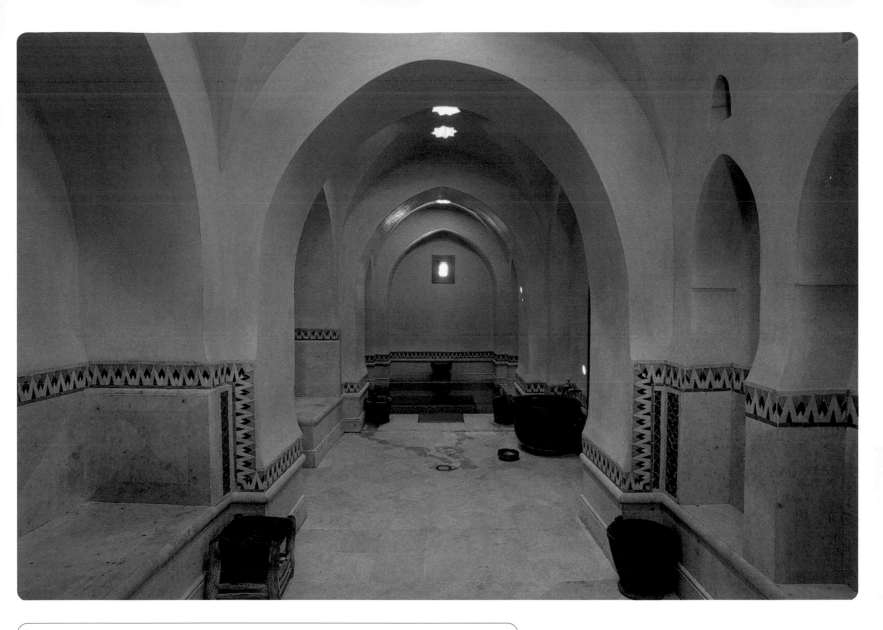

A series of niches structures the areas where one can sit and enjoy conversation with a certain discretion and intimacy.

Left: The magnificent enclosed garden, connected to the sitting room which adjoins the hamam. Below: Detail of the superb studded door of hundred-year old wood with its finely-carved frame.

In the sitting room adjacent to the water area, where one can go to relax, the ceiling is lined with laurel wood handcrafted using an ancient pre-Saharan technique.

Hidden under a thick climbing plant, a hundred year old wooden door leads us to a refined hamam where the materials take the spotlight. Stone, wood, and an intense blue gresite with flecks of gold, combine to create a charming space.

EASTERN ESSENCE

Location: **Majorca, Spain**
Surface area: **64 sq. ft.**

An old building, where years ago the peasants of Majorca kept their farming tools, was chosen as the location for this water area. Some of these vestiges of the past have been integrated into this space as benches or towel racks. But the most spectacular part of this project is the perfect combination of the original stone structure and the chromaticity of the flooring. This intense contrast has made it possible to integrate the small interior pool and the central channel without visually altering the formal surface of the floor.

A prominent feature is the line traced between the two side walls by a small central channel that continues visually in a vertical fashion on the thick stone wall, creating an effect of the side walls coming together. The same effect is achieved by the double play of light, one natural and the other artificial and underwater, between both surfaces.

The walls, more than three feet thick, support a vaulted ceiling, which the droplets from the dense steam slide down. Two rustic benches and a simple wooden hanger complete the restrained setting, conducive to relaxation, where the ritual of water and steam constitute the authentic essence of the hamam.

A small channel of water cuts down the central part of the room in a vertical line along the perpendicular walls, bringing about their visual union.

The thickness of the walls keeps the hamam's interior hot. The vaulted ceiling enables the water droplets produced by the steam to slide down to the floor.

Some equipment that was previously used for agricultural work has been recycled for the decoration of this setting.

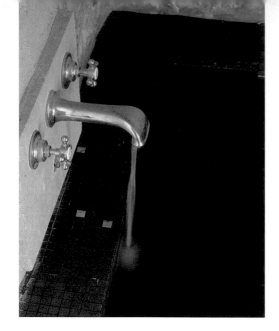

Above: Detail of the magnificent bronze fixture. Below: A point of light placed strategically in the water of the small channel, just below the fixture on the wall.

The two rustic benches and the various wooden accessories were recovered from among the farming equipment kept in this old building adjacent to the main house.

Pool designers:

Eli Mouyal (*Pool in introduction*)
Wolf Siegfried Wagner (*A mirror between the earth and sky*)
Tomas Wegner (*Inspired by the past*)
B&B W Estudio de arquitectura. Sergi Bastidas, Wolf Siegfried Wagner (*Color contrasts*)
B&B W Estudio de arquitectura. Sergi Bastidas, Wolf Siegfried Wagner (*Nomadic sensations*)
B&B W Estudio de arquitectura. Sergi Bastidas, Wolf Siegfried Wagner (*The eternal cycle of water*)
Marco Emili (*The color turquoise*)
Ramon Esteve, architect (*Recovering the past*)
Juan de los Ríos, architect (*A stream amid the rocks*)
Erwin Bechtold (*Private space*)
Christopher Travena (*Rural symmetry*)
Rolf Blackstad, architect (*The patina of time*)
Françoise Pialoux (*Vantage point*)
Bruno, Alexandre & Dominique Lafourcade (*Classical spirit*)
Guillem Mas, engineer (*Between two worlds*)
Aranda, Pigem, Vilalta Arquitectes (*Minimalist character*)
Tomas Wegner (*Oriental essence*)
Bruno, Alexandre & Dominique Lafourcade (*Classical personality*)
Bruno Lafforgue (*Carved in stone*)
Patrick Genard, architect (*Exercise in contrasts*)
Àngels G. Giró & Luis Vidal (*Chromatic personality*)
Lluís Alonso and Sergi Balaguer Arquitectos Asociados (design), XYZ Piscinas (project) (*Zen symmetry*)
Charles Boccara, architect (*The reinterpretation of water*)
Guillermo Maluenda Colomer, architect (*In the hearth of a quarry*)
Josep Armenter i Arimany, technical architect and coordination and
Charles Boccara, architect (*Traditional inspiration*)
Charles Boccara, architect (*In the shade of a palm grove*)
Charles Boccara, architect (*The value of the past*)
Charles Boccara, architect (*Sensorial space*)
Víctor Espósito (*Textures and forms,* in this page)

The authors would like to pay special thanks to the homeowners for opening their doors, to the architects for their creativity, and to the following people and groups for their help and collaboration during the development of the stories.

Rafael Calparsoro, Xavier Farré, José Gandia, Nona von Haeften, Laure Jakobiack, Gabriel Vicens and Mamen Zotes, Jean Paul Lance & Jalal Alwidadi, Olivia Vidal & Mercedes Echevarria, Unicorn and Coconut Company (Majorca, Spain), Gandia Blasco SA (Valencia, Spain), Hotel Les Terrasses (Ibiza, Spain), Hotel Lindos Huéspedes (Pals, Spain), Mas de l'Ange (Mollégés, France), Hotel Les Deux Tours (Marrakech, Morocco).

And:
Antonia & Tomeu, Christian, Bern, Alexandra, Cecilia, Bernadette, Maria, Carmen & Manolo, Nuria, Olivier, Carlos, Danielle & Susan, Said, Aicha, Mohamed, Nassima, Chris, Clay & Annie, Nora, Stanislas.